READING STREET

Responsibility

Program Authors

Connie Juel, Ph.D.

Jeanne R. Paratore, Ed.D.

Deborah Simmons, Ph.D.

Sharon Vaughn, Ph.D.

Glenview, Illinois
Boston, Massachusetts
Chandler, Arizona
Upper Saddle River, New Jersey

ISBN-13: 978-0-328-45278-1
ISBN-10:   0-328-45278-5

9 10 V011 14 13
CC1

Responsibility

2

Contents

Good Job!

See page 33 for My New Words!

5

Good Job!

Many people have jobs. They work hard each day and try their best. Jobs can be at small shops or in big stores. Jobs can be inside buildings or out in sunshine. People work at lots and lots of jobs.

Some have jobs driving trucks. They drive big trucks across many miles. These trucks are filled with all sorts of things that we need.

What might be inside this big truck?

These workers make cars. Each big car is made of smaller parts.

Each worker makes one part. Some make seat belts. Some make hubcaps. Some make taillights.

The workers must be sure that parts fit just right. What might happen if someone forgot a piece? What might happen if someone did not place it in just the right spot?

These workers fix streets and roads. Listen!
Have you heard them drilling?

Look! Have you seen them waving red flags?
They hold these flags up high so that cars will
see them and not drive fast.

10

Black tar is used to patch potholes and get rid of cracks in roads.

We all like to ride on nice streets and roads and highways. What if these did not get fixed right? What might happen to cars' tires?

Kids can do jobs at home. Your job might be to read your sister a silly book at bedtime. It might be to pack a lunchbox, dry dishes, make beds, or take out cans.

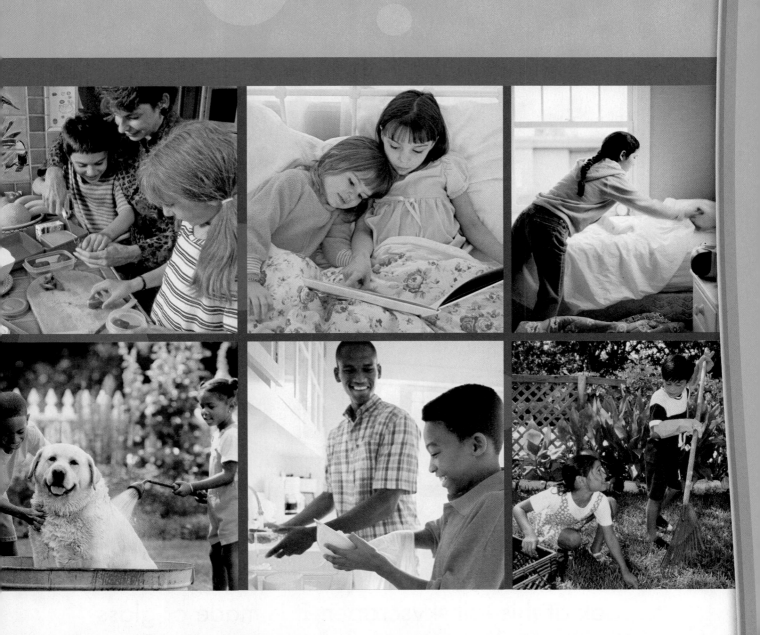

Moms and dads like kids to help them with big jobs and small jobs. What jobs do you do at home?

SOARING SKYSCR

Look at this tall skyscraper. It is made of glass and steel. It rises up and up and up.

We must bend our necks to see its top. It seems to scrape the sky. In fact, that is how it got its name.

APERS

It is a big job to make something this huge. It takes lots of planning, time, and people. Each step is important. Each step must be done just right.

The first step is to make plans. These plans are called blueprints. They tell how long and high walls need to be.

Workers must make each wall the right size. It is not hard for workers to read these plans. It is as easy as reading a book.

Workers start at sunrise. They dig a deep hole. Then they make platforms to sit on or stand on. Cranes lift steel beams and put them into place. Steel beams form a frame, piece by piece.

Skilled workers drive pickup trucks, dump trucks, cement trucks, and cranes. Have you heard these big machines? Thump! Screech! Whir! They can make the land shake!

What machine is this?

Brave workers walk up high on thin beams.
It is like walking on tightropes in a circus.

Hard hats help keep workers safe. Belts hold
things like hammers and drills.

Work places buzz like beehives.
People on sidewalks peek in holes. Each day they spot new things. They listen as machines squeak and purr. Thump, bang, screech!

Just one person cannot make this huge skyscraper. It takes lots of workers to get each step done. Think about this the next time you see buildings that seem to scrape the sky!

THREE SMALL FROGS

by Maria Vasquez • illustrated by Joe Kulka

Once there were three small frogs. Each
frog made a home to live in. The first small frog
made his home out of pads that float on ponds.
   One day Snake came to his home and yelled,
"Small Frog, Small Frog, let me in."

The first small frog sang, "No, no, no, not by the green of my chin, chin, chin."

Snake yelled, "Then I'll huff and I'll hiss, and I'll blow your home in."

Snake huffed, and he hissed, and the home fell in.

The first small frog hopped to the home of the next small frog. The next small frog made her home out of cattails.

The first small frog cried, "Listen! It's Snake!"

Along came Snake. He yelled, "Small Frog, Small Frog, let me in."

The next small frog sang, "No, no, no, not by the green of my chin, chin, chin."

"Then I'll huff and I'll hiss and I'll blow your home in," yelled Snake.

Snake huffed, and he hissed, and the home fell in.

The first small frog and the next small frog
hopped to the home of the last small frog. The
last small frog made his home out of bricks.

The last small frog was sitting on his big,
homemade rug. He heard the frogs outside.

"Come in!" the last small frog called.
"I'm reading my book. It's not bedtime yet."
The two small frogs cried, "Help! Our homes
are in pieces! Snake is coming!"
The last small frog said, "My home is made
with bricks. He can't get us!"

Then they heard Snake say, "Small Frog, Small Frog, let me in."

"No, no, no, not by the green of my chin, chin, chin," sang the last small frog.

"Then I'll huff, and I'll hiss, and I'll blow your home in," yelled Snake.

Well, Snake huffed, and he hissed, and he huffed, and he hissed, but the home didn't fall in. This made Snake very upset.

The three frogs heard Snake get on top of the home. He was going to slide inside! But the last small frog had a plan.

He made a fire in the fireplace. Then he got a big pot that could hold lots of water. He set it on the fire.

Snake fell into the hot water, and that was the last thing he ever did!

Rhyme and RIDDLE

If your best pal is sick,
And he is your pet,
I can make him better.
I am a _____!

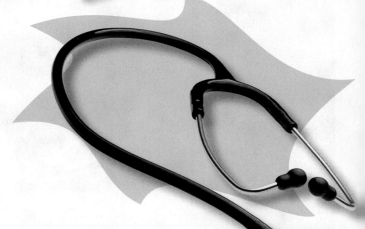

I will save you from danger.
I rhyme with *brighter*.
I use a ladder.
I am a _____!

I like to find rocks.
I explore space a lot.
I visit the moon.
I am an _____!

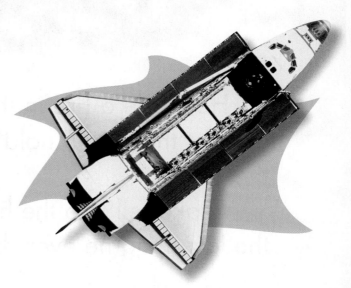

Answers: vet, firefighter, astronaut

My New Words

book*

This **book** has many pictures.

cattail

A **cattail** is a tall plant with a long, furry, brown spike on top.

heard*

I **heard** the noise.

hold*

Will you **hold** my hat? That jug can **hold** a lot of water.

listen*

When you **listen**, you try to hear something or someone.

piece*

I lost a **piece** of the puzzle.

worker

A **worker** is a person who does a job.

*tested high-frequency words

Contents

Family Jobs

See page 68 for My New Words!

Family Jobs

This is the Brown family. They live on the
south side of town in a brick townhouse.
Mom and Dad go to work. The kids go
to school. But the house must be kept clean.
Who will keep this house clean and neat?

A year ago, the Browns made a plan that each person in this family would help out by doing jobs in the house. Since they all live in this house, they all must help.

Let's find out how each person will help.

This is Mom. Mom's job this day is to mop the kitchen tile. She fills a pail with hot, soapy water. Then she dips the mop in the pail and scrubs the tile.

Wow! Mom helps out her family by mopping.

This is Dad. Dad's job this day is to fix a broken pipe down under the sink. He pounds and pounds.

"I am certain this new pipe will not break," Dad thinks.

Wow! Dad helps out his family by fixing a pipe.

This is Jeff. Jeff is sixteen years old. His job this day is to vacuum. He makes sure the carpets are clean. It is a loud job!

Wow! Jeff helps out his family by vacuuming.

This is Scout. Scout is ten years old. Her job this day is to dust the round table by the couch. She sprays the table and wipes it down.

Wow! Scout helps out her family by dusting.

This is Krissy. Krissy is just five years old.
Krissy's job this day is to feed Mister Howl.
Mister Howl probably wishes he could have
more chow.

Wow! Krissy helps out her family by feeding
Mister Howl.

This is Mister Howl. Mister Howl's job this day is to make the Brown family smile. They smile when Mister Howl wags his tail. They smile when he licks their cheeks.

Bow wow! Mister Howl helps out his family by making them smile.

The Brown family is happy to do jobs that help keep their house neat and clean. Mom and Dad, Jeff, Scout, and Krissy all help out. Mister Howl helps out too.

What jobs do you have at your house? How do you help out?

TOOLS
for You and Me

by Christopher Talbot

All families use tools that help with jobs around the house. These things help save time and make jobs easier.

People from long ago used tools to help with jobs too. They made tools with stones, twigs, branches, and animal bones.

harpoon

mallet

Those tools were quite simple and could break easily. But they were very useful.

Tools have changed a lot since that time. Today we crowd our closets and sheds with helpful tools.

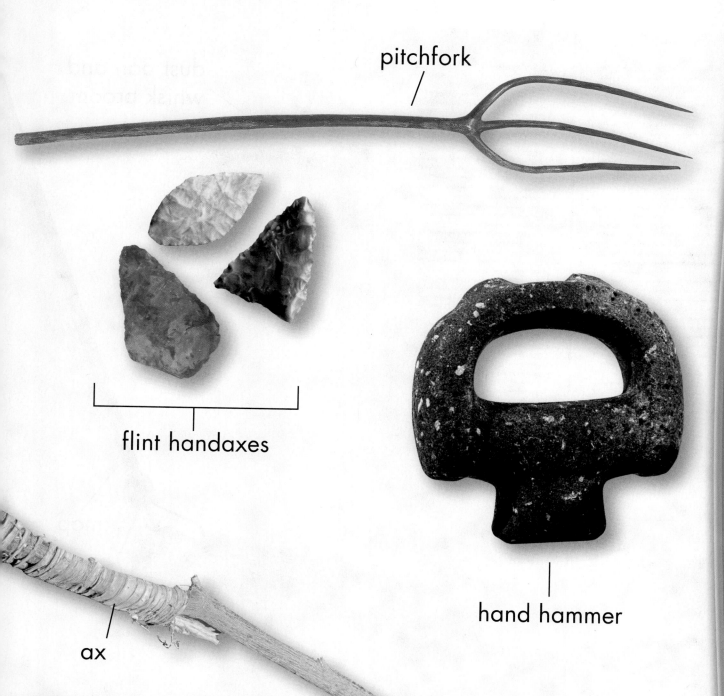

pitchfork

flint handaxes

hand hammer

ax

Look closely at these tools. They help with inside chores. Answer these riddles.

This has a long handle with yarn or cloth strips at its end. It cleans dirty grime or nasty spills. What is it? Yes! It is a mop.

dust pan and whisk broom

mop

This is powerful and mainly sucks up dust hidden in rugs. It makes loud sounds when it is turned on. What is it? Yes! It is a vacuum cleaner.

feather duster

vacuum cleaner

pail and sponge

Look closely at these tools. They are helpful with outside jobs. Answer these riddles.

This has a long handle with spikes that look like teeth. It is used for gently gathering leaves. What is it? Yes! It is a rake.

wheelbarrow

This looks like a tightly twisted snake. We use it to lightly squirt water on flowers and grass. What is it? Yes! It is a hose.

hose

rake

lawnmower

We all use tools that help us with chores. You probably have many things like these at home. We must be certain to use these things correctly. And we need to be careful to put them back neatly.

Mops, vacuums, rakes, and hoses are quite helpful. What other tools are useful?

Counting on Tess

by Mona Taylor
illustrated by Elizabeth Allen

Tess was on pins and needles. She could hardly wait! Today her family was going on a camping trip. She had counted down the days since the end of June.

"Have you started packing?" asked Mom.
"There isn't much time."

"You can count on me," said Tess proudly.
"This time I'm making a list. If I don't, I will
probably forget something."

"Let's see," mumbled Tess as she curled
up on her bed. "I need shorts, shirts, and
sandals for sunny days. Some days might be
cloudy. I'll take my raincoat and books in case
of showers."

Tess jotted down each thing in her notebook. Then she stretched.

"This is so hard," she sighed. "I'm really tired. I think I'll take a quick nap." Tess dozed off.

Meanwhile, Dad and Max scrubbed the van and hosed it down with water.

"I'm certain I just cleaned this van a week ago," moaned Dad. "Thanks for helping, Max. By the way, where's Tess?"

"I think she's packing," replied Max. "Maybe this time she won't need our help. I'm glad that she's packing by herself."

Grandmom was hard at work too. She put
peanuts in bags for snacks. She cut up cheese.
She even baked a spice cake.

"Mmm…what is that good smell?" asked
Max brightly. "It's time for a break."

"I certainly thought Tess would be here in a flash when she smelled cake," laughed Grandmom.

"She's packing," said Max as he grabbed an apple and dashed back outside.

Mom found tents and sleeping bags and set them on the grass. She quickly stuffed blankets in huge brown bags.

"I wish Tess would be more helpful," thought Mom out loud. "But I'm grateful that she is packing. I'm glad we can count on her to pack her bag by herself."

While Tess slept soundly, her family buzzed
around like bees. Dad and Max packed the van.
Mom dropped off the dog at a neighbor's house.
Grandmom quickly watered the houseplants.
Mom's loud call woke up Tess.

"It's time to go, Tess!" she shouted. "Are you all set?"

Tess sprang up in bed and rubbed her eyes. "No, no!" she howled. "How could this happen? I still have lots to pack! Don't worry, Mom! You can count on me—but next time!"

Make a Chores

One way busy families can remember their chores is to make a chores calendar. Here's how.

- Get construction paper, markers, and a ruler.
- Look at a calendar for this month. Copy it.

MAY

Sunday	Monday	Tuesday
		YOKO Return library books
KEN and YOKO help Mom wash car 6	7	
	KEN Set the table	

66

Calendar

- In each space, write each family member's chore for that day.
- Decorate the calendar.
- Place the calendar where everyone in the family can see it, such as on the refrigerator.

...nesday	Thursday	Friday	Saturday
			KEN and YOKO give Rover a bath 5
	KEN Weed flower boxes 3	4	
2		YOKO Water plants 11	KEN Clean hamster cage 12
...KO ...ean fish ...owl 9	10		
		KEN and YOKO Clean bedrooms 18	
16	17		19

My New Words

ago* If it happened long **ago**, it happened in the past.

break* When you **break** something, you make it fall to pieces or stop working. A **break** is also a short period of rest.

certain* If you are **certain** about something, you are very sure. **Certain** can also mean some but not all. Only **certain** trees grow here.

probably* You **probably** know my brother.

since* I have been up **since** 6:00. **Since** you are hungry, we can eat.

*tested high-frequency words

tools   **Tools** are things that help you do work.

vacuum   To **vacuum** means to clean something with a vacuum cleaner.

Contents

Taking Care of Animals

See page 103 for My New Words!

Taking Care of ANIMALS

Boys and girls often ask moms and dads for pets. Pets can be lots of fun, and they make good pals. It makes kids feel good to have something of their own to care for.

It is not always that simple to take care of them. Pets can be hard work. Pets need to be fed and kept clean. Some pets need several walks a day. Others need you to play with them lots.

Dogs can make nice pets. Dogs can take long walks and snuggle on fluffy rugs. Dogs like fetching balls too. But you might end up throwing a ball a hundred times before that dog gets tired!

Dogs need their fur brushed to keep it soft and shiny. Dogs with long fur can get tangles if it is not brushed.

This might be the best time to give your dirty pet that bath it needs. But run fast if that dog starts shaking itself dry, or you might get soaked!

Cats can make nice pets too. They like to cuddle on laps, but be gentle when you're holding them.

Cats like poking their noses in open paper bags and other odd places. Keep an eye on your cat. It likes to hide.

Cats like to play with plastic balls that have little bells inside. You can slide a ball to your cat. The bell jingles as the ball slides. Then the cat pats the ball and slides it back to you.

If kids need smaller pets, gerbils can make nice pets. They seem cute with those noses that wiggle! Gerbils can live in either wire or glass cages.

Each day give your gerbil fresh water and something to nibble. And clean that cage at least one time each week.

Birds can make nice pets too. They make us smile with their bright colors and sweet songs. Birds need wire cages with lots of space.

Birds like shiny things that dangle. You can hang these things in the cage for your bird to play with. Some birds can even learn to talk. That will make you giggle!

Which pet do you think you could care for?

Safe Places

by Anna Perez

Many kids own pet cats and dogs. But lots of cats and dogs don't have homes. These dogs and cats are called strays. Life is not easy for them. They must struggle to survive. Who will help keep them safe?

for Strays

Most cities have places for stray pets. These places are called shelters. Workers at shelters feed and take care of lost dogs and cats. They scramble to find homes for these pets. This is not as simple as it seems. But all pets need safe homes.

Shelters need lots of workers. Some workers don't get paid. They give time and help for free. They help because they like dogs and cats and hope to make life better for these pets.

Vets may make visits to shelters each week. Vets handle the animals with care and help them if they are sick.

Workers and vets hope boys and girls will take home either a dog or cat. All pets need stable homes!

Bad storms can flatten homes. Then dogs and cats have no place to live. Workers try to save these pets. They may bring several hundred lost dogs and cats back to shelters. Workers must be gentle. They try not to startle these sad, stray pets.

Sometimes shelters take stray dogs and cats to shopping malls. Workers walk around malls with these cute little dogs and cats. They try to get moms, dads, and kids to stop and cradle them. They hope families will take them home as pets.

Shelters may hold classes on training pets. Kids can learn how to walk puppies on a leash. And old dogs can learn new tricks! Workers can teach dogs how to sit, stay, and come.

You're lucky if you have a pet dog or cat. And your pet is lucky too. But if you're thinking of getting a dog or cat, check out a shelter for pets. All pets need happy homes!

Snuggles
and
Cuddles

by Lauren Alexander
illustrated by Fred Willingham

I am Gimble Gomez, reporting live from Snuggles and Cuddles Shelter. Let's peek in this window before we go inside.

See that furry little face? See that happy tail? Hear that bark?

That's what you can see and hear at
Snuggles and Cuddles Shelter. This is the place
where lots of sweet, cute dogs and cats wait for
new homes.

When a family wishes to get a pet, they visit Snuggles and Cuddles Shelter. At this shelter, they can pick either a dog or a cat. Then they can take their new pet home.

Who are these cats and dogs? Let's meet
several and learn their stories.

Freckles is a beagle. Freckles was quite
little when someone found him and gave him
to the shelter.

Vets fed him bottles of fresh milk. Freckles got
bigger and stronger.

This little boy just came in. His name is
Caleb. Caleb is meeting Freckles. Caleb likes it
when Freckles wiggles and wobbles.

"You're so sweet and cute!" cries Caleb. "I'll
take care of you!" Look! Freckles is leaving the
shelter with his new family.

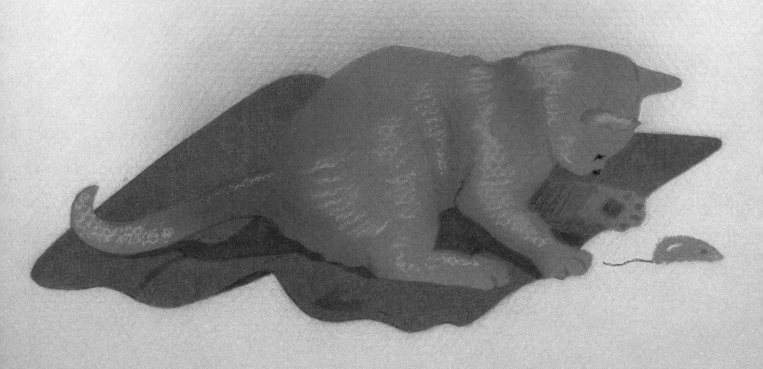

Spunky is a frisky, gray cat. Spunky was lost
in the middle of the night. A man spotted him
and gave him to the shelter.

Vets let Spunky settle on a bundle of blankets.
They fed him until he got stronger.

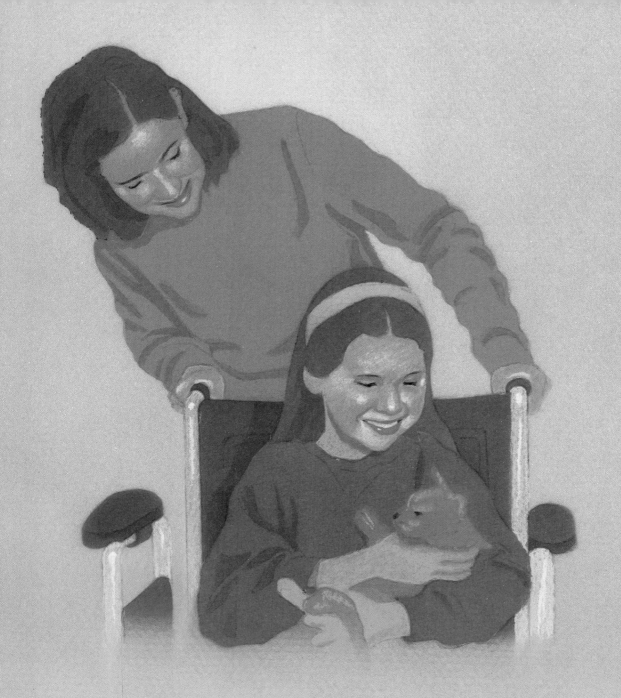

This little girl is Amber. She is meeting Spunky. Amber likes it when Spunky stretches and tumbles.

"You're so sweet and cute!" cries Amber. "I'll take care of you!" And Spunky is leaving the shelter with his new family.

Babe is a big, old dog. At one time, Babe ran and played. She splashed in puddles and chased rabbits by the maple trees. But now Babe is not able to run that fast.

Someone dropped Babe off at the shelter. Vets fed her until she felt better.

Here is a lady in a bright purple coat. She is meeting Babe. She likes it when this big, old dog licks her hand. She likes Babe's soft, gentle eyes. "You're so sweet and cute," she whispers to Babe. "I'll take care of you. Let's go home."

Yes, there are hundreds of sweet, cute dogs and cats that wait for new homes at Snuggles and Cuddles Shelter.

But now there are three fewer!
I am Gimble Gomez, saying good night from
Snuggles and Cuddles Shelter.

THE MONSTER'S PET

by Lilian Moore • illustrated by Jeff Shelly

What kind of pet
Would a monster get
If a monster set
His mind on a pet?

Would it snuffle and wuffle
Or snackle and snore?
Would it slither and dither
Or rattle and roar?

Would it dribble and bribble
In manner horr-rible
Or squibble and squirm
Like a worm?

And every day
In pleasant weather,
Would they go out
For a walk together?

My New Words

beagle   A **beagle** is a small dog with smooth, short hair and drooping ears.

boy*   A **boy** is a male child.

dangle   The cat played with the string that **dangled** in front of it.

either*   Choose **either** of these two toys to give to the baby.

hundred*   One **hundred** is the number after ninety-nine.

several*   **Several** means more than two or three but not many.

stable   Something that is **stable** does not change.

you're*   **You're** is a short way to write *you are*. **You're** very funny.

*tested high-frequency words

Contents

My Neighbors, My Friends

See page 127 for My New Words!

My Neighbors, My Friends

Great things happen when neighbors work together. This is a nice neighborhood. But it needs a playground. Kids need a safe and fun place to spend time.

These people meet and talk about things that might be needed. They will ask the whole neighborhood to pitch in and help.

Of course, this project will not be easy. It will take time. But it will be fun too.

People of all ages meet one weekend. Some
bring tool chests and paintbrushes. Some dig
holes or lift beams. Others work on slides,
swings, and sandboxes.

Every person is thrilled with how well the playground turns out. Great things can happen when many people help.

Neighbors and friends plan to have a big picnic soon!

They all meet at noon on a cool day. The park is crowded with happy people. Cam's brother makes goofy things with balloons. Brad's sister juggles balls.

Each person brings food. Hot dogs! Corn on the cob! Scoops of homemade ice cream!

Kids zoom on shiny bikes and scoot down sidewalks on skates. Moms and dads enjoy chatting with friends.

Soon it is time to go home. But every person knows that this time together has been very special!

What Makes a

by Stuart Mitchell

    People live in different places. Some live on
peaceful country roads. Some live on loud city
streets. Of course, no matter where people live,
they all have neighbors.

    What makes a nice neighbor?

Nice Neighbor?

Kim thinks nice neighbors help out when Mom can't.

Kim lives in a big city. Her mom is unable to drive her home after school. So Miss King picks her up. When Kim is sick, her buddy Todd drops off her homework.

Cooper thinks nice neighbors are friendly.

Cooper lives just outside a big city. His neighbors smile and wave at Cooper when he is outside. When Cooper is unhappy, Kaitlin and Scott cheer him up.

Abby thinks nice neighbors help each other. Abby lives on this farm in the country. Lindy and James helped Abby and her dad unload hay. And then Sam and Brent spent a whole day helping repaint the barn.

Kelly thinks nice neighbors are like family.
Kelly lives in a small town. Unlike some kids,
Kelly has no brothers or sisters. But her neighbor,
David, is just like her brother. Kelly and David
have been special pals for a long time. These
kids play games and retell silly jokes.

Lucky thinks nice neighbors take long walks. Lucky is a big dog that lives with Ellen in a city. When Ellen is unable to walk him, Travis will get Lucky's leash and unlock his gate. Travis takes Lucky for long walks.

The Twins Next Door

by Samantha Roberts
illustrated by Guy Francis

Miss Boon peeks outside. She checks the time on her clock. It's time for Devin and his twin brother, Cole, to stop by. Devin and Cole are Miss Boon's neighbors. They are her special friends too. Each weekend they stop by to help her with chores.

"Devin and Cole will get here soon. Will they ring the bell or play a trick?" Miss Boon asks herself. "I bet it will be a trick."

Then Miss Boon hears light scratching. "Is a mouse in my house?" she grins.

"No," a twin whispers. "Try again."

Miss Boon asks, "Is a raccoon snooping? Who is it? I'm unable to guess!"

"Boo!" Devin and Cole say as they rush into the room. "Did we fool you? Did you like our spooky trick? Did we get here on time?"

"Yes, you have been on time each weekend," Miss Boon tells the twins. "It is noon. But now unzip those jackets. Let's get started on these jobs. Then we can play a fun game."

"Devin can unpack those messy boxes. Cole can refill these jars with rice. And then we can all unload stuff that is in my car."

The twins unpack, refill, and unload. Nothing is left unfinished.

"Now can we play that game?" begs Devin.

"Of course we can," smiles Miss Boon. "But let's reread the rules first."

After the game they munch on a whole bowl of popcorn. Then Devin and Cole set out for home.

"Thanks for your help," Miss Boon calls.

She walks back in and stops. "Do I hear mice in my house?" asks Miss Boon. "Yes," yell the twins. "And they'll be back soon!"

How Does Jack Get to School?

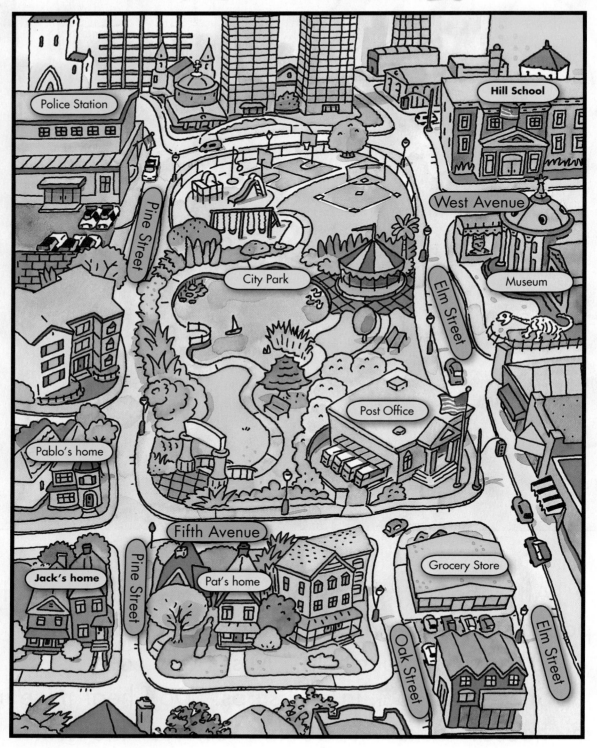

Find the shortest way for Jack to get to school from his home.

My New Words

been*   This boy has **been** here for hours.

brother*   Your **brother** is a boy or man with the same parents as you.

course*   Of **course**, we can go!

neighborhood   Your **neighborhood** is the streets and houses around where you live.

snoop   To **snoop** means to sneak and look around.

special*   Your birthday is a **special** day.

whole*   Something that is **whole** is in one piece.

*tested high-frequency words

Contents

Doing the Right Thing

See page 159 for My New Words!

Let's Find Out

Doing the

Kids just like you have to make choices each day. Should we pick up toys or just leave a mess? Should we help Mom and Dad or play with pals? Should we watch and wait to cross streets or just run across without looking?

Right Thing

Each day we ask, "What is the right thing to do?" Read these stories. Then think about what choices must be made.

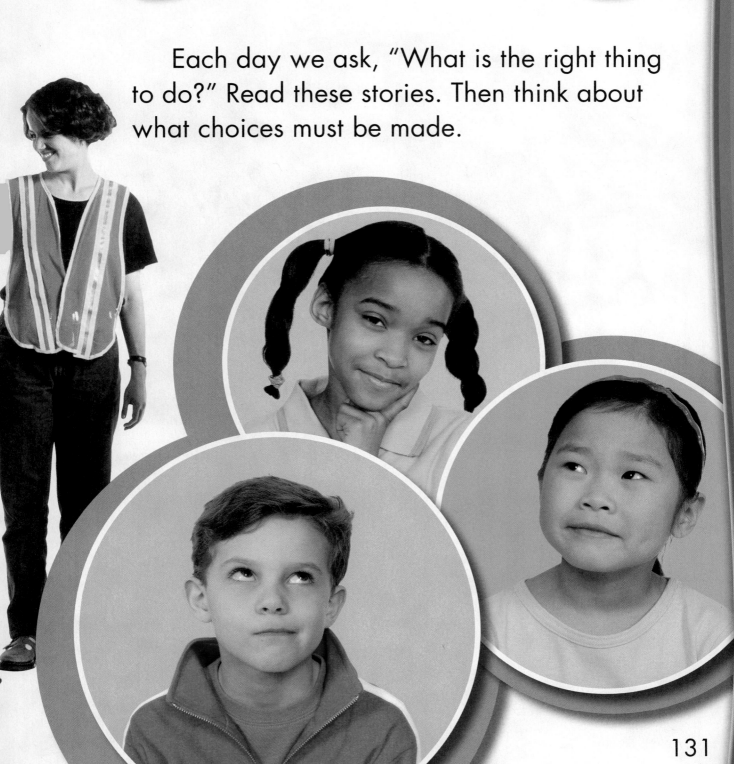

Mom is planning a surprise birthday party for Dad. Mom tells Joy not to tell Dad the party plans. That will spoil the surprise for Dad. But it's so hard for Joy not to tell!

Joy must think long and hard. She thinks Dad will enjoy his party more if it is a surprise. She will be sorry if she tells the secret. Will Joy make a good choice?

At the park, Troy spies a small bag on the ground. It has many coins inside. Wow! He can use these coins to get treats or toys. Troy picks up the bag and puts it in his pocket.

Minutes later, a little girl at the park tells Troy she dropped a bag of coins. She asks Troy whether he has seen it. What will he say? Will Troy make a good choice?

Kids get noisy playing in Jing's backyard. Boys and girls scream and shout. Their voices are loud! Lots of Jing's pals join in.

Now it's getting late and neighbors don't like this loud noise. They ask kids to stop playing.

But these kids want to play for at least an hour more. They are having too much fun! What is the right thing to do? Will Jing and her pals make a good choice?

When was the last time you made a choice? Did you do the right thing?

Who Teaches Us Rules?

by Cara Martinez

Many people teach us rules. They help us follow them too. Do you know who teaches rules? Do you follow these rules?

teacher

nurse

firefighter

bus driver

police officer

This man drives kids to and from school on his bus. He tells kids to sit down in their seats. He asks kids not to scream or wriggle. He knows his bus rules help boys and girls stay safe.

This person enjoys helping kids learn. He knows good rules will help his class. He tells kids to raise their hands. He tells them to walk, not run, down halls.

He tells kids to write neatly. They must watch out for wrong answers and fix them. Kids in class must follow these rules to be safe and to do well in school.

This nurse teaches kids how to stay safe on the school playground. But sometimes kids scrape a knee, sprain a wrist, or twist a thumb. She fixes them up and calls Mom or Dad if kids get hurt.

She teaches kids to eat well and to get enough hours of sleep each night. She cares about all kids.

This man puts out fires. He also visits classrooms and spends many minutes talking about rules to prevent fires. He teaches kids how to be smart and safe in case of fire. He shows kids how to safely leave a burning building.

This person helps keep our city safe. She points out rules she wants us to know. She tells us to ride on bike paths and to use seat belts in cars. She doesn't want us to make bad choices that will make us feel sorry.

No Rules Day

by Micah Joy   illustrated by Barry Gott

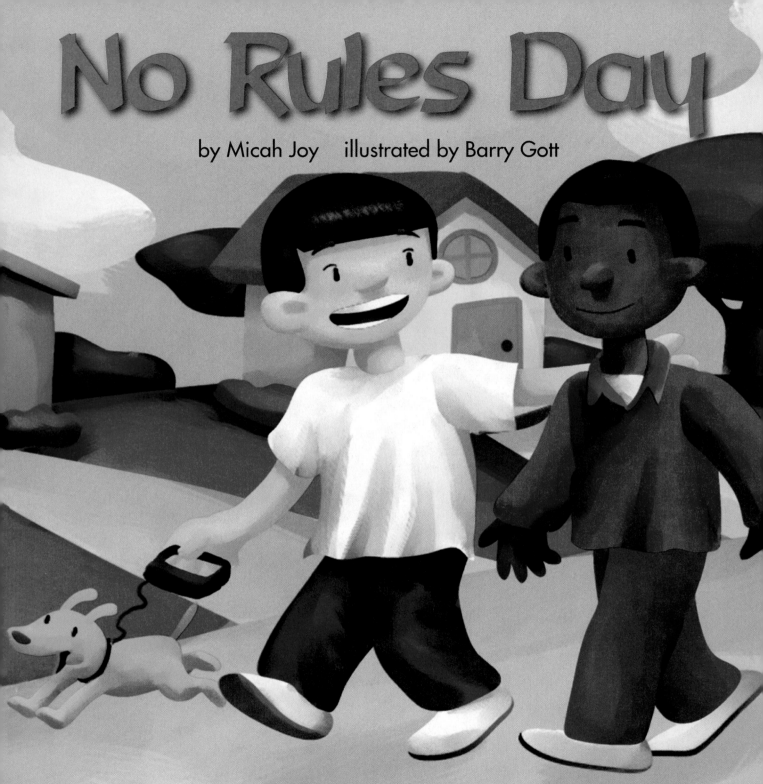

Roy is a good boy. He helps Mom and Dad with a joyful smile. He cleans his knife, fork, and plate after meals. He walks his dog, Loyal. He never bugs his pals. And he follows every rule.

But this morning, Roy gets up on the wrong side of the bed. He decides that rules are a bore. "I'm tired of always following rules," he thinks. "Rules aren't that important. I am not going to follow them at all today! And I won't be sorry!"

147

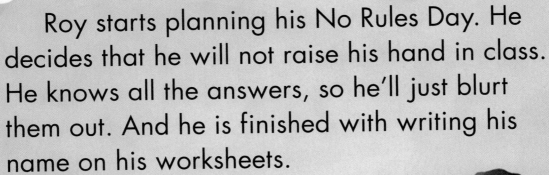

Roy starts planning his No Rules Day. He decides that he will not raise his hand in class. He knows all the answers, so he'll just blurt them out. And he is finished with writing his name on his worksheets.

Roy plans to eat only what he likes at lunch hour. He will leave his trash and won't get rid of crumbs on the table. Why should he care how the lunchroom looks?

He decides not to put away his toys before dinner. That might take too long. Cleaning up would spoil his playtime! And it hurts his knees to kneel and pick up all those little pieces.

And he won't hang up his shirts or pants. Who cares if they get wrinkled?

Roy keeps thinking up more rules that he will not follow. No Rules Day will be a day to enjoy! He can't wait.

Roy washes his face, brushes his teeth,
and puts on his sneakers. He wants to
look his best for No Rules Day.
    As he stuffs his books in his knapsack,
he hears a voice in the hall.

Then the knob turns and a funny king walks in.
"I didn't knock," the king tells Roy, "because
you decided there will be no rules."
"Who are you?" asks Roy.

"I'm the King of Rules," shouts this funny king. "And I rule. Just watch what might happen in a land without rules!"

The King of Rules shows Roy what might happen. Cars screech by fast and get into wrecks. A noisy classroom is filled with rude kids. Messy lunchrooms are brimming with trash. A boy's bedroom is piled high with junk.

After a while, the King of Rules looks at Roy. "What do you think, Roy?" he asks. "Do you think it is wrong to have rules?"

Roy thinks for a minute. Then he starts to put his toys away. He picks up his shirts and pants and hangs them up. What do you think Roy said?

FUNNY Laws

In **Florida**, if you tie your elephant to a parking meter, you must put money in the meter.

In **Minnesota**, you may not cross into another state with a duck on your head.

In Chicago, **Illinois**, you can't fish from a giraffe's neck.

In **New York**, you may not walk with an ice-cream cone in your pocket on Sundays.

158

My New Words

hour*

An **hour** is a unit of time. There are 60 minutes in one **hour**.

knapsack

A **knapsack** is a cloth bag with two shoulder straps, similar to a backpack.

leave*

When you **leave**, you go away.

minute*

A **minute** is one of the 60 equal parts of an hour.

A **minute** is 60 seconds.

sorry*

Someone who is **sorry** feels sad about something.

watch*

When you **watch** something, you look at it for a while.

wriggle

When you **wriggle**, you twist and turn.

*tested high-frequency words

Acknowledgments

Text

Every effort has been made to locate the copyright owner of material reproduced in this component. Omissions brought to our attention will be corrected in subsequent editions. Grateful acknowledgment is made to the following for copyrighted material.

102 Marian Reiner, Literary Agent "The Monster's Pet" by Lilian Moore from *Spooky Rhymes and Riddles*. Copyright © 1972 by Lilian Moore. Used by permission of Marian Reiner.

Illustrations

Cover: Jeff Shelly, Guy Francis; **5, 22–31** Joe Kulka; **35–45** Karen Stormer Brooks; **54–65** Elizabeth Allen; **90–101** Fred Willingham; **102** Jeff Shelly; **106–111** Linda Pierce; **118–125** Guy Francis; **126** Randy Chewning; **129, 146–157** Barry Gott; **133–137** Janet McDonnell; **158** Rémy Simard.

Photographs

Every effort has been made to secure permission and provide appropriate credit for photographic material. The publisher deeply regrets any omission and pledges to correct errors called to its attention in subsequent editions.

Unless otherwise acknowledged, all photographs are the property of Pearson Education, Inc.

Photo locators denoted as follows: Top (T), Center (C), Bottom (B), Left (L), Right (R), Background (Bkgd)

Cover: (CL) ©Ariel Skelley/Corbis, (CR) ©Royalty-Free/Corbis, (BR) Getty Images; **1** (CL) ©Ariel Skelley/Corbis; **2** ©Ronnie Kaufman/Corbis; **4** (C) ©Natalie Fobes/Corbis; **5** (TR) ©Royalty-Free/Corbis; **6** (BCR) ©LWA- JDC/Corbis, (TCL) ©Mika/Zefa/Corbis, (TC) ©Ronnie Kaufman/Corbis, (TCR) ©Royalty-Free/Corbis, (BC) ©Tim Wright/Corbis, (BCL) ©Walter Hodges/Getty Images; **7** (C) ©Royalty-Free/Corbis; **8** (C) ©Danny Lehman/Corbis; **9** (BCR, BC) ©Andy Sacks/Getty Images, (BCL) ©China Features/Sygma/Corbis, (TCL) ©Danny Lehman/Corbis, (TC) ©David Joel/Getty Images, (TCR) ©Pete Leonard/Corbis; **10** (B) ©AbleStock/Index Open, (TCR) ©Brent Stirton/Getty Images, (BCR) ©Jorgen Schytte/Peter Arnold, Inc., (TCL, TC) ©Michael Newman/PhotoEdit, (BCL) ©Robert Brenner/PhotoEdit, (BC) Getty Images; **11** (C) ©Thomas Mayer/Peter Arnold, Inc.; **12** (C) ©Peter Beck/Corbis; **13** (BCL) ©Ariel Skelley/Corbis, (TCL) ©Bill Aron/PhotoEdit, (BCR) ©Robert E Daemmrich/Getty Images, (TC, BC) ©Royalty-Free/Corbis, (TCR) Getty Images; **14** (C) ©Pixtal/SuperStock, ©Robert Llewellyn/Zefa/Corbis, (Bkgd) ©Royalty-Free/Corbis; **15** (TC) ©Robert Llewellyn/Zefa/Corbis, (C) DK Images; **16** (C) ©Gandee Vasan/Getty Images, (TC) ©Robert Llewellyn/Zefa/Corbis, (Bkgd) ©Royalty-Free/Corbis; **17** (TC) ©Robert Llewellyn/Zefa/Corbis, (C) ©Susan Van Etten/PhotoEdit; **18** (TC) ©Robert Llewellyn/Zefa/Corbis, (Bkgd) ©Royalty-Free/Corbis, (C) Getty Images; **19** (C) ©Natalie Fobes/Corbis, (TC) ©Robert Llewellyn/Zefa/Corbis; **20** (C) ©Monika Graff/The Image Works, Inc., (TC) ©Robert Llewellyn/Zefa/Corbis, (Bkgd) ©Royalty-Free/Corbis; **21** (TC) ©Robert Llewellyn/Zefa/Corbis, (C) ©Royalty-Free/Corbis; **32** (TCR, CL, BCR) Getty Images; **46** (CL) ©Colin Keates/Natural History Museum, London/DK Images, (BL) ©Michael J. Doolittle/Peter Arnold, Inc., (BC) ©Peter Hayman/The British Museum/DK Images; **47** (C) ©Dave King/DK Images, (TC) ©Geoff Brightling/DK Images, (CL) ©Maurice Nimmo; Frank Lane Picture Agency/Corbis, (BR) ©Werner Forman/Corbis; **48** (R, L, C) Getty Images; **49** (BR, BL) Getty Images, (CL) Stockdisc; **50** (B) ©Brad Simmons/Getty Images; **51** (T) ©Richard Hutchings/Corbis, (BL) ©Royalty-Free/Corbis, (C) Getty Images; **52** (B) ©Richard Hutchings/Corbis; **53** (BL) ©Cathy Melloan, (BR) ©Masaaki Toyoura/Getty Images, (C) ©Simon Watson/Getty Images; **70** (C) Getty Images; **71** (TR, CR) ©Henry Horenstein/Corbis; **72** (TR) ©Frank Greenaway/©DK Images, (TL, CR, CL, C) ©Royalty-Free/Corbis; **73** (C) ©Ariel Skelley/Corbis; **74** (C) ©tstockphoto/Fotolia; **75** (C) ©Ariel Skelley/Corbis; **76** (C) ©GK & Vikki Hart/Getty Images; **77** (C) DK Images; **78** (C) ©Dennie Cody/Getty Images; **80** (C) ©Juniors Bildarchiv/Alamy Images; **81** (C) ©Arco Images/Alamy Images; **82** (BC) ©Henry Horenstein/Corbis; **83** (C) ©Steven Clevenger/Corbis; **84** (C) ©Don Ryan/AP/Wide World Photos; **85** (CL) ©Royalty-Free/Corbis, (CR) Courtesy of PAWS Chicago; **86** (C) ©Don Ryan/AP/Wide World Photos; **87** (C) ©Richard Hutchings/Photo Researchers, Inc.; **88** (C) ©Don Ryan/AP/Wide World Photos; **89** (C) Getty Images; **104** (C) ©Paul Barton/Corbis; **105** (CR) ©Sonya Etchison/Fotolia; **112** (TL) ©Charles E. Rotkin/Corbis, (TR) ©Jason Hawkes/Getty Images; **113** (C) ©Michael Newman/PhotoEdit; **114** (C) ©Royalty-Free/Corbis; **115** (Inset) ©Cathy Melloan/PhotoEdit, (T) ©John and Eliza Forder/Getty Images; **116** (C) ©Paul Barton/Corbis; **117** (C) ©Sonya Etchison/Fotolia; **128** (C) Getty Images; **129** (TR) R. Lord/Image Works; **130** (BL) ©Lisa M Robinson/Getty Images; **131** (CR) Getty Images; **132** (C) ©Richard T. Nowitz; **134** (C) Getty Images; **136** (C) ©Fernando Bueno/Getty Images; **138** (CR) ©Michael Newman/PhotoEdit, (BC) Blend Images/Getty Images, (BL) Corbis, (CL) Getty Images, (BR) R. Lord/Image Works; **139** (Bkgd) ©Mike Siluk /The Image Works, Inc., (BR) Blend Images/Getty Images; **140** (C) Getty Images; **141** (R) Getty Images; **142** (L) ©Michael Newman/PhotoEdit; **143** (C) ©Michael Newman/PhotoEdit; **144** (C) ©Bill Stormont/Corbis, (CL) Corbis; **145** (C) ©Richard Lord/The Image Works, Inc., (BR) R. Lord/Image Works.